ULTIMATE IRON MAN VOL. 1. Contains material originally published in magazine form as ULTIMATE IRON MAN #1-5. First printing 2006. ISBN# 0-7851-1499-8. Published by MARVEL PUBLISHING, INC., a subsidiary of MARVEL ENTERTAINMENT, INC. OFFICE OF PUBLICATION: 417 5th Avenue, New York, NY 10016. Copyright © 2005 and 2006 Marvel Characters, Inc. All rights reserved. $14.99 per copy in the U.S. and $15.75 in Canada (GST #R127032852); Canadian Agreement #40668537. All characters featured in this issue and the distinctive names and likenesses thereof, and all related indicia are trademarks of Marvel Characters, Inc. No similarity between any of the names, characters, persons, and/or institutions in this magazine with those of any living or dead person or institution is intended, and any such similarity which may exist is purely coincidental. **Printed in Canada.** ALAN FINE, CEO Marvel Toys & Publishing Divisions and CMO Marvel Entertainment, Inc.; DAVID GABRIEL, SVP of Publishing Sales & Circulation; DAVID BOGART, SVP of Business Affairs & Talent Management; MICHAEL PASCIULLO, VP of Merchandising & Communications; JIM O'KEEFE, VP of Operations & Logistics; DAN CARR, Executive Director of Publishing Technology; JUSTIN F. GABRIE, Director of Editorial Operations; SUSAN CRESPI, Editorial Operations Manager; OMAR OTIEKU, Production Manager; STAN LEE, Chairman Emeritus. For information regarding advertising in Marvel Comics or on Marvel.com, please contact Mitch Dane, Advertising Director, at mdane@marvel.com. For Marvel subscription inquiries, please call 800-217-9158.

10 9 8 7 6 5 4 3 2 1

ULTIMATE IRON MAN

WRITER:
ORSON SCOTT CARD

PENCILS:
ANDY KUBERT AND MARK BAGLEY

INKS: DANNY MIKI
WITH BATT, JESSE DELPERDANG, JOHN DELL & SCOTT KOBLISH
COLORS: RICHARD ISANOVE
WITH DAVE MCCAIG & LAURA MARTIN
LETTERS: CHRIS ELIOPOULOS
ASSISTANT EDITOR: SEAN RYAN
EDITOR: NICK LOWE
CONSULTING EDITORS: RALPH MACCHIO & MIKE MARTS

COLLECTION EDITOR: JENNIFER GRÜNWALD
ASSISTANT EDITOR: MICHAEL SHORT
SENIOR EDITOR, SPECIAL PROJECTS: JEFF YOUNGQUIST
VICE PRESIDENT OF SALES: DAVID GABRIEL
PRODUCTION: JERRY KALINOWSKI
BOOK DESIGNER: JEOF VITA
VICE PRESIDENT OF CREATIVE: TOM MARVELLI

EDITOR IN CHIEF: JOE QUESADA
PUBLISHER: DAN BUCKLEY

ISSUE 01

Dr. Cerrera, welcome to Stark Defense Corp.

I'm Howard Stark.

On TV you looked taller.

I've been losing height.

You had something to show me?

Not even a bruise. What *is* that stuff?

Armor.

Go wash that off before it eats too much of your skin.

So that blue paste-- it's alive?

It can only be spread through the blood. I could kiss her and I wouldn't catch it. I've got everything we know about the virus here.

The virus was designed for monkeys. Who knows what it will do to humans?

I deserve whatever it does to me. But the baby?

If the choice is up to me...we can have other babies.

If I lost *you*, I'd never find you again.

Idiots who get infected with a virus they designed themselves are a dime a dozen.

I'm sorry, Howard. You have to sign these papers to make the settlement with Loni final.

Stane Corporation Headquarters

So did you bring me that wedding present?

I got all the stock we need.

You get control of Stark Defense Corporation...

And you get me.

No pain. I've been hitting myself with hammers, putting my hands in candle flames, nothing hurts.

How long this time?

A week. Only the outer layer of skin is eaten away.

So if the skin regenerated only a little faster...

I think this batch might work on your--

ISSUE 02

He was ready for us. But he couldn't have known I was buying up his stock!

Why not? *I* did.

Bio-Armor *is* required to provide Stark Corporation with samples.

We can have our own scientists analyze them and figure out how to make more.

You really don't know anything about science, do you, darling?

The samples won't tell you the process they used to create them.

That's why Howard never patents anything. You have to reveal the process.

You played me.

You said we'd *get* his patents.

I'm being kidnapped! Help!

You're in so much trouble you wouldn't believe how much trouble!

What happened to taping his mouth?

The tape kept dissolving.

I covered his mouth while I got him away from the house.

Go wash before that stuff eats your whole arm off.

Nobody's going to hurt you, Tony. We just need a sample of that blue stuff you've got all over you.

Sedate him.

My father will find you and blow you all up!

Your father doesn't even know you're missing.

ISSUE 03

Okay, who's next?

He isn't even bleeding.

There isn't even a bruise.

Okay, guys. Two more times, and then I get to do it to you.

What about *my* turn? A deal's a deal!

Now it's my turn!

Hey!

I don't know *what* you are.

And I don't know why you're so unbreakable.

But I'm *not* unbreakable, and now you've set me up!

If you're thinking of joining the football team, they'll never let you use that on the field.

It's a prototype. For a whole suit of armor.

You've *got* armor. *Subtle* armor.

I want armor that stops them *before* they throw me around.

That secret government school for geniuses that Loni wants to send her boy to. Why didn't you send *me* there?

I don't want them to hold you back. I don't even want them to know you exist.

ISSUE 04

Thanks for calling me instead of 9-1-1.

Tony told us to.

He was conscious?

Through everything.

Good job, Tony.

New skin over everything. Already.

If the muscles weren't so atrophied, you'd never know there'd been an injury.

No gurney.

I'm walking out of here.

You can't.

I can in the suit.

ISSUE 05

How many of these do we have to wreck before you start trying it on thinner sheets of steel?

Why don't I just use sheets of paper? Then I'd succeed every time.

All right, Nifara, everything's set. Do it.

This resonance-imaging thing just isn't working, Rhodey.

Wait. It's still ringing.

Wow. You've discovered the gong.

Sorry I'm late, gentlemen.

Late? You aren't expected here, Tony.

Call my father, if you please.

My father's proxy for the voting stock, which, combined with my shares, represents one hundred percent.

My father's nomination of myself as a board member, and his nomination of myself as acting chairman and chief executive officer until his return from prison.

And his certification that the stock has been voted accordingly, in a meeting of stockholders that he and I held in the visiting room, with a notary and an attorney present to record the meetings.

You're under age. Will any contracts you enter into be legally binding?

Dad also issued a statement that as my guardian, he is responsible for all my debts and contracts.

I think it's time for me to be brought up to speed on all the operations of Stark Enterprises. Ryan, will you please report on personal weapons development?

Bill, you can sit down now. Your report on pending negotiations will be next.

Of course, Mr. Stark.

Of course, Mr. Stark.

All your previous instructions from my father are still in force, but I expect you to take the initiative in telling me when those decisions need to be reviewed.

I'll be in my father's office every morning from seven till nine.

After that, look for me in my own lab. I expect you to interrupt me at need.

Obadiah denies everything, of course. And the prosecutor is quite candid about being able to destroy Rhodes and Nifara on cross.

Biased witnesses who owe you everything. And Obadiah is the victim's son.

So all we've got is the blood of an unidentified killer.

They're calling him your "assistant."

You think they've got enough to convict?

They taped your whole session in the autopsy room. The fact that you knew they would have a single hair can work for you or against you.

The jury won't like the way you came up with an exact design for the murder weapon on the spot.

Si Ma, I'm going to be here for a while, apparently.

I need you to look after Tony for me.

HOWARD STARK

They've got enough to hold you till the trial.

He's running a corporation, and he needs a babysitter?

Good morning, Tony.

Uh...Mr. Stark. Your messages are waiting on your desk.

All passengers move to the front of the ferry. Now! Get away from the rear of the boat!

TO BE CONTINUED

ISSUE 01
VARIANT

pg.1 thumbnail

ROUGH CUT:
ULTIMATE IRON MAN #1
SCENE ONE

PAGE ONE

Pic 1; AERIAL VIEW: Long Island Sound between the Bronx and Queens. Rising out of the water is the Stark Defense Corporation plant. Domes on stilts, like tied-down bubbles. The domes are hardened for explosion containment, so there are no windows except in a single spire-like office tower in the middle. A fast launch is cutting across the water from Stark Pier in Queens to the plant.

CAPTION: Stark Defense Corporation
Headquarters New York City

CAPTION 2:   Years Ago...

Pic 2; The launch is at a landing platform among the stilts. HOWARD STARK, a tall wiry man in his forties, wearing a 1980s suit, reaches out to help MARIA CERRERA, a frail-looking Latina woman of thirty, make the leap onto the dock.

HOWARD: Dr. Cerrera, Welcome to Stark Defense Corp.

Pic 3; She stands a little too close to him, so that, tall as he is, she has her head thrown back to look up at him, and he's looking way down at her.

HOWARD: I'm Howard Stark.

MARIA: On TV you looked taller.

HOWARD: I've been losing height.

Pic 4; HOWARD'S POV: Maria gazes up at him. She may be wearing a business suit, but it doesn't hide that she's a woman.

MARIA: You had something to show me?

PAGE TWO

Pic 1; Inside a testing lab. A bare-chested young man is being sprayed by a female lab technician, Si Ma, with what looks like sky-blue paint. Howard and Maria are watching.

Pic 2; Howard is holding up an ice pick.

HOWARD: Here. Stick him with this.

Pic 3; Maria takes the ice pick, frowning.

MARIA: Stick him where?

HOWARD: Wherever.

Pic 4; Maria pushes it against the blue-painted man's arm.

HOWARD (OFF): Come on, put
some weight
behind it.

Pic 5; The ice pick goes part way in, the skin dimpling under
the pressure.

HOWARD (OFF): Harder.

Pic 6; The ice pick is in his arm up to the handle.
Maria looks at Blue Man.

MARIA: Doesn't that hurt?

pg.2 thumbnail

Pic 7; Blue-painted man looks at her blandly.

BLUE MAN: Ouch.

Pic 8; Blue Man grins.

PAGE THREE

Pic 1; Maria pulls out the ice pick. Only there's no shaft anymore. The metal
looks more like a Brillo pad or a pom-pom — wiry twists of very thin metal
going every which way.

Pic 2; Maria holds up the ice pick to show Howard.

MARIA: That blue stuff — it can
do this to metal, and it
doesn't hurt his skin?

pg.3 thumbnail

HOWARD: Not for the first
fifteen minutes.

Pic 3; Howard picks up a wooden baseball bat.

Pic 4; He rares back to let fly at Blue Man's chest.

BLUE MAN: I hate this part.

Pic 5; The bat connects with his chest.

Pic 6; Blue man flies backward.

HOWARD: Lift off!

PAGE FOUR

Pic 1; Blue Man is sprawled on the floor.

Pic 2; The lab technician dips a sponge into a pan and wipes off the blue stuff, baring the skin on Blue Man's chest.

Pic 3; Maria kneels by him, examining him.

MARIA: Not even a bruise. What is that stuff?

BLUE MAN: Armor.

Pic 4; Howard helps Blue Man to his feet.

HOWARD: Go wash that off before it eats too much of your skin.

Pic 5; As Blue Man and the lab technician leave, Maria and Howard watch.

MARIA: So that blue paste — it's alive?

PAGE FIVE

Pic 1; Howard inserts a cassette into a Betamax.

Pic 2; In a conference room, Howard and Maria watch a picture of swirling sky-blue microbes on the TV screen.

HOWARD: Bacteria. They live on the surface of the skin.

MARIA: Eating skin cells?

HOWARD: Only when they're hungry.

Pic 3; CLOSEUP of the microbes. Little tendrils link them together.

HOWARD: Here's what happens when something hits them.

Pic 4; CLOSEUP of the microbes. They suddenly reorient and reshape themselves, long and thin now, and radiating outward from a center point.

HOWARD: They spread the shock of impact outward. The guy still flies across the room, but it's as if the bat were a big soft hand pushing him.

Pic 5; Maria gazes at the brillo-ended ice pick.

MARIA:　That still doesn't explain this.

Pic 6; Closeup of a single bacterium. Now we see that the tendrils are covered with tiny globules.

HOWARD:　Our bacterium has a parasite. Those little globules are like piranha, only instead of flesh, they eat metal.

MARIA:　Any metal?

HOWARD:　Not gold. But any metal that can oxidize.

PAGE SIX

Pic 1; Howard turns off the projector.

MARIA:　So you've reinvented armor.

HOWARD:　Still have a few problems.

Pic 2; Howard leads the way out of the conference room.

HOWARD:　It won't stop a bullet. Moving too fast.

Pic 3; Howard leads the way along an outside corridor, only a railing between them and the Long Island Sound far below.

HOWARD:　And after about three hours, it eats away all your skin.

Pic 4; Howard leans on the railing, looking out toward New York City in the distance, to the southwest. Maria is looking at Howard.

pg.6 thumbnail

MARIA:　So if you're attacked with ice picks and baseball bats...

HOWARD:　You're invulnerable. As long as you have soap and water close by.

Pic 5; Maria grins at him.

MARIA:　And it's such a lovely color.

HOWARD:　Sky blue. Goes with everything.

ISSUE ONE
COVER
VARIANT #1
PENCIL ROUGH

moon/
night
sky

ISSUE ONE
COVER
VARIANT #2
PENCIL ROUGH

ISSUE ONE: COVER VARIANT #1
FINAL PENCILS

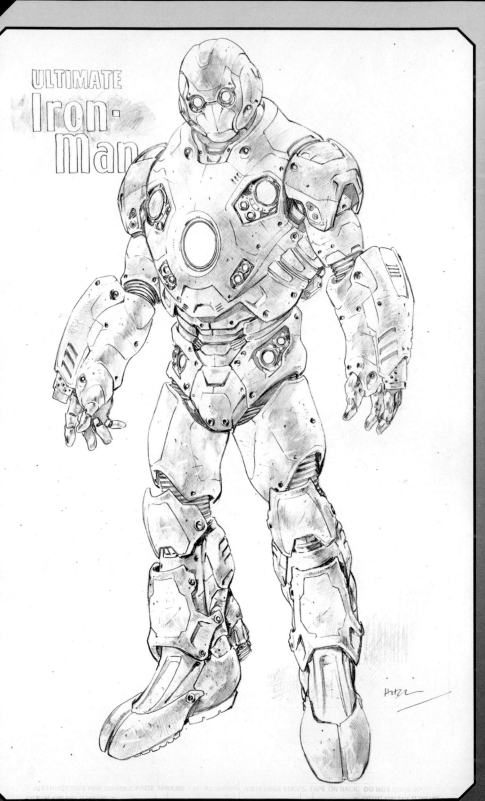

ULTIMATE
Iron·
Man

IRON MAN
ARMOR CONCEPT

UNUSED COVER LAYOUTS

ISSUE #2
COVER PROCESS

**ORIGINAL
THUMBNAIL**

**ORIGINAL
THUMBNAIL**

**FINAL
LAYOUT**

FINAL PENCILS

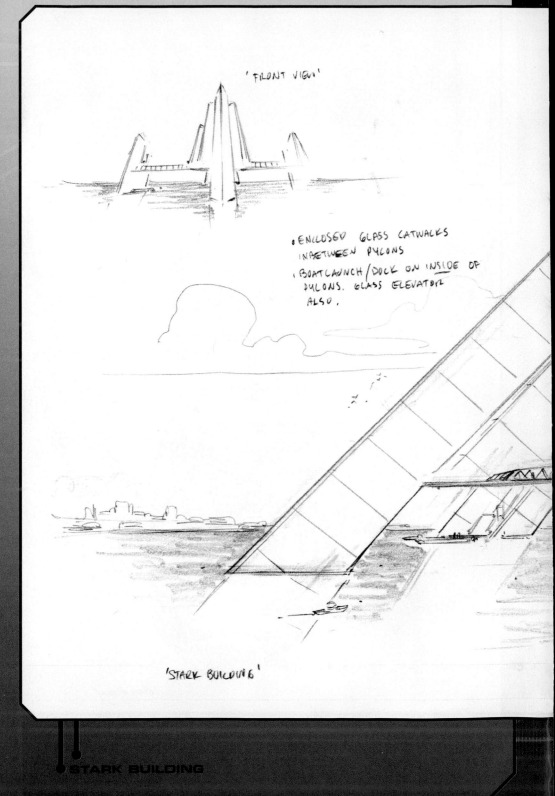

'FRONT VIEW'

• ENCLOSED GLASS CATWALKS
  INBETWEEN PYLONS
• BOATLAUNCH/DOCK ON INSIDE OF
  PYLONS. GLASS ELEVATOR
  ALSO.

'STARK BUILDING'

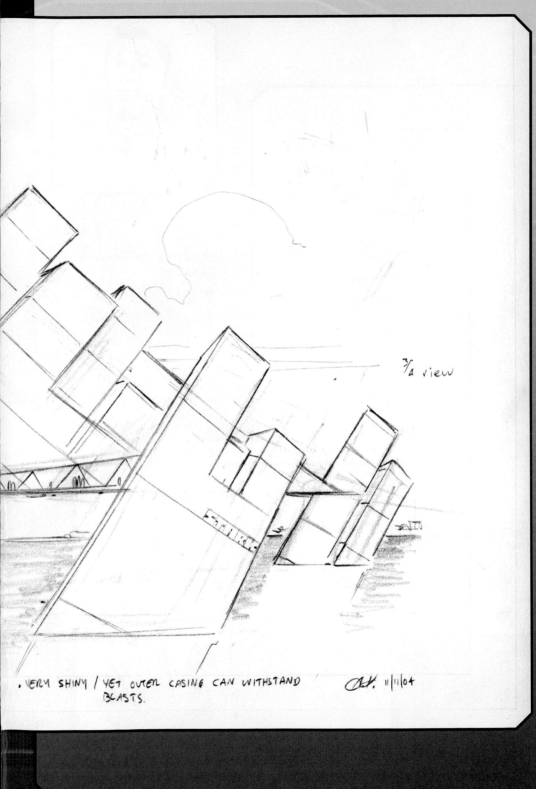

³/₄ view

. VERY SHINY / YET OUTER CASING CAN WITHSTAND
     BLASTS.   11/11/04

'MARIA COLLERA'

80's HAIR
'DARK HAIR'

'THIN'

HOWARD
STARK

ORIGINAL
CONCEPT ART
BY ANDY KUBERT

MARIA
STARK

• HOWARD HUGHES
  LIKE
• BIG 80's GLASSES

HISTORY: Blessed and cursed with extraordinary genius, Tony Stark is the son of inventor and defense contractor Howard Stark, and geneticist Maria Stark. The Starks were developing a biological personal armor coating when a lab accident with a regenerative virus fatally infected Maria. The virus mutated her unborn child, Tony, growing additional neural tissue throughout his body which augmented his intelligence while causing chronic pain. Maria died, but Howard saved Tony by coating him in their bacterial bio-armor, which consumed ordinary skin but not Tony's constantly regenerating neural flesh. Business rival Zebediah Stane married Howard's scheming ex-wife Loni, with whom he stole Stark's company, and spent years trying to seize the bio-armor. As a teenager, Tony befriended fellow prep school student Jim Rhodes and began developing his own "Iron Man" armor technology. Becoming a wealthy celebrity and science prodigy, young Tony founded multi-billion dollar design and manufacturing corporation Stark International. He also became an infamous playboy, alcoholic, and womanizer, suffering from recurring depression and secretly learning he was dying from an inoperable brain tumor.

Later, Stark would claim he developed the armor. When he and his shifty cousin Morgan were taken hostage along with other civilians by Guatemalan guerrilla terrorists, their captors demanded Stark's technology in exchange for the hostages' freedom. They killed Morgan when Tony refused to cooperate. Pretending to acquiesce, Stark built makeshift armor and defeated the terrorists with it. Years later, Stark used new Iron Man armor to save the President from an assassination attempt, becoming a bigger celebrity than ever, but refusing to sell or mass-produce his armor technology. When Latverian ambassador Golog tried to steal Stark's "Irontech" with the covert approval of intelligence agency S.H.I.E.L.D., Stark fought off Golog's Mandroids with the aid of Spider-Man. Spurred by his

REAL NAME: Antonio "Tony" Stark
KNOWN ALIASES: Monopoly Man
IDENTITY: Publicly known
OCCUPATION: Inventor, CEO, U.S. government super-operative
CITIZENSHIP: U.S.A.
PLACE OF BIRTH: Unrevealed
KNOWN RELATIVES: Howard & Maria Cerrera Stark (parents, deceased), Morgan Stark (cousin, deceased), Antonio (uncle, deceased), uncle (name unrevealed, deceased)
GROUP AFFILIATION: Ultimates, Stark Industries
EDUCATION: Multiple scientific doctorates, studied at Harvard and MIT
FIRST APPEARANCE: Ultimate Marvel Team-Up #4 (2001)

tumor to make the most of his remaining days, Stark joined the Ultimates, a S.H.I.E.L.D.-sponsored superhero team. Forming an unlikely friendship with anti-corporate teammate Thor, Stark helped defeat the Hulk, the Chitauri and others. Dating teammate Natasha Romanov (Black Widow), Tony eventually proposed to her, creating new armor for her as an engagement gift; however, when a super-army conquered the team, Natasha suddenly attacked Tony, placing him — and their relationship — in jeopardy.

HEIGHT: (unarmored) 6'1", (armored) 7'
WEIGHT: (unarmored) 225 lbs., (armored) 2000 lbs.
EYES: Blue
HAIR: Black

ABILITIES AND ACCESSORIES: Tony Stark is a phenomenal scientific genius and inventor, thanks largely to his body-wide neural tissue, which enhances his intelligence and gives his body fantastic regenerative capacity. His bacterial bio-armor fits his body like a second skin, enhances his durability, and inhibits his chronic neurological pain. He is multilingual, has nearly total recall, and has a seemingly limitless capacity for multitasking. His Iron Man armor grants him tremendous superhuman strength and durability, enabling both supersonic flight and submersible travel, and houses repulsor rays, a uni-beam, mind-impairing "thought-scramblers," "light-negativity" devices allowing short-term invisibility, force field generators, a tracking system, communications tech and onboard computers. He can manually recharge his armor from outside sources or draw additional power from a network of dedicated satellites.

POWER GRID	1	2	3	4	5	6	7
INTELLIGENCE							
STRENGTH							
SPEED							
DURABILITY							
ENERGY PROJECTION							
FIGHTING SKILLS							

THE ULTIMATES

ACTIVE MEMBERS: Black Widow (Natasha Romanov), Captain America (Steve Rogers), Hawkeye (Clint Barton), Iron Man (Tony Stark), Quicksilver (Pietro Maximoff), Scarlet Witch (Wanda Maximoff), Wasp (Janet Pym)
FORMER MEMBERS: Giant-Man (Hank Pym), Hulk (Bruce Banner), Lieberman (deceased reservist), Thor (allegedly Thorlief Golman)
RESERVES: The Four Seasons, the Goliaths, Intangi-Girl, Owen, O'Donohue, Rocketman One (Dexter), Rocketman Two, Rocketman Three, Rusk, Son of Satan (Damien), Thunderbolt, unspecified others
BASE OF OPERATIONS: The Triskelion, Upper Bay, Manhattan
FIRST APPEARANCE: Ultimates #2 (2002)

HISTORY: The world's foremost superhuman strike force, the Ultimates trace their origins back to World War II super-operative Captain America (Steve Rogers), whom the U.S. government empowered in part to oppose the Nazis' secret extraterrestrial Chitauri allies. Rogers appeared to die while helping destroy the Chitauri/Nazi war effort, and U.S. scientists tried for decades to duplicate his powers. In recent years, the super-soldier program's lead scientist was geneticist Bruce Banner, reporting to General Ross, head of the S.H.I.E.L.D. intelligence agency. Later, new S.H.I.E.L.D. director Nick Fury pushed through a multi-billion expansion of the super-soldier program, though Banner's temporary transformation into the monstrous Hulk resulted in his demotion to deputy under new head scientists Hank and Janet Pym, who did double duty as size-changing super-operatives Giant-Man and Wasp. Altruistic armored billionaire inventor Tony Stark soon joined as Iron Man. Enigmatic left-wing powerhouse Thor refused membership at first, but Captain America himself was found alive and revived from a state of suspended animation to join the team. Together, Rogers, Stark and the Pyms became the Ultimates, headquartered in the high-tech Triskelion complex and backed by a huge support staff, a large conventional military force and black ops agents. Banner's semi-estranged girlfriend Betty Ross (daughter of General Ross) was hired as Director of Communications and helped make the new team into celebrities while making Bruce's life miserable. The depressed Banner finally snapped and transformed into the Hulk again, embarking on a destructive rampage stopped by the Ultimates with the aid of Thor, who began working with the team thereafter.

The Hulk's true identity was concealed from the public, and the Ultimates became beloved national heroes. The group soon expanded: intelligence veterans Hawkeye and Black Widow and mutant ex-terrorists Quicksilver and Scarlet Witch were promoted from the black ops division to the core team. Meanwhile, Hank Pym nearly killed his wife during a violent domestic dispute and was himself beaten into traction by Captain America, who later began dating the Wasp. Pym's former assistant Dr. Eamonn Brankin became the new scientific head of the program. Despite losing Giant-Man, the Ultimates saved the world from a Chitauri plot with the unwitting aid of the Hulk and became bigger icons than ever. They went on to apprehend Kraven, Electro, Luther Manning, the X-Men and Norman Osborn's "Six." Later allied with the European Super-Solider Initiative, the Ultimates became more controversial as they began operating in foreign territory, notably the Middle East. Thor quit, and a traitor within the group outed Banner as the Hulk. Seemingly executed for the Hulk's crimes, Banner secretly survived with the aid of Hank Pym, who was soon fired from the Ultimates altogether. Meanwhile, apparently exposed as a madman, Thor was brutally arrested by the team. The global community grew wary as the Ultimates developed many more superagents as their reserves, and anti-Ultimates sentiment accelerated when the team stripped a small "rogue" Middle Eastern nation of its nuclear capability. The traitor within the Ultimates responded by murdering Hawkeye's family, framing Captain America for the crime, and helping a foreign super-army invade America. Assisted by Hank Pym, this foreign force destroyed the Triskelion and occupied major American cities, slaughtering the reserves and capturing the remaining Ultimates in the process.

Art by Bryan Hitch